1 PIANO, 4 HANDS

PIANO DUET PLAY·ALONG
VOLUME 14

Boublil and Schönberg's

LES MISÉRABLES

Music by Claude-Michel Schönberg
Lyrics by Herbert Kretzmer
Original French Lyrics by Alain Boublil and Jean-Marc Natel

CONTENTS

PLAYBACK+
Speed • Pitch • Balance • Loop

To access audio, visit:
www.halleonard.com/mylibrary

Enter Code
5269-3643-2176-2359

Dramatic Performance Rights
controlled and licensed by
Cameron Mackintosh (Overseas) Ltd.
One Bedford Square,
London WC1B 3RA England
Tel (20) 7637 8866 Fax (20) 7436 2683

Stock and Amateur Performance Rights
are licensed by
Music Theater International, Inc.
545 Eighth Avenue,
New York, New York 10018
Tel (212) 868-6668 Fax (212) 643-8465

Non-Dramatic and Concert Performance Rights
are controlled by Alain Boublil Music Ltd.
and licensed by the American Society of
Composers, Authors and Publishers (ASCAP),
One Lincoln Plaza,
New York, New York 10023
Tel (212) 595-3050 Fax (212) 787-1381

ALAIN BOUBLIL MUSIC LTD.
c/o Joel Faden and Company Inc.
1775 Broadway, New York, NY 10019

ISBN 978-1-4234-5204-1

Visit Hal Leonard Online at
www.halleonard.com

Contact Us:
Hal Leonard
7777 West Bluemound Road
Milwaukee, WI 53213
Email: info@halleonard.com

In Europe contact:
Hal Leonard Europe Limited
Distribution Centre, Newmarket Road
Bury St Edmunds, Suffolk, IP33 3YB
Email: info@halleonardeurope.com

In Australia contact:
Hal Leonard Australia Pty. Ltd.
4 Lentara Court
Cheltenham, Victoria, 3192 Australia
Email: info@halleonard.com.au

BRING HIM HOME

SECONDO

Music by CLAUDE-MICHEL SCHÖNBERG
Lyrics by HERBERT KRETZMER and ALAIN BOUBLIL

Moderately

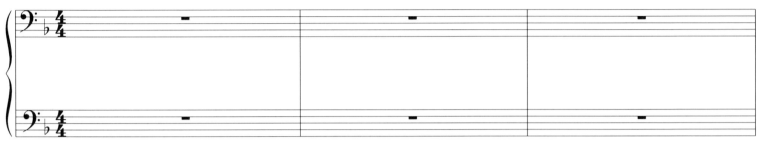

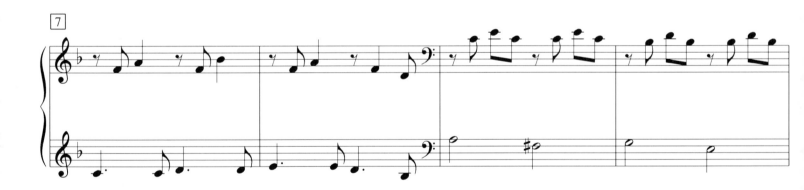

BRING HIM HOME

PRIMO

Music by CLAUDE-MICHEL SCHÖNBERG
Lyrics by HERBERT KRETZMER and ALAIN BOUBLIL

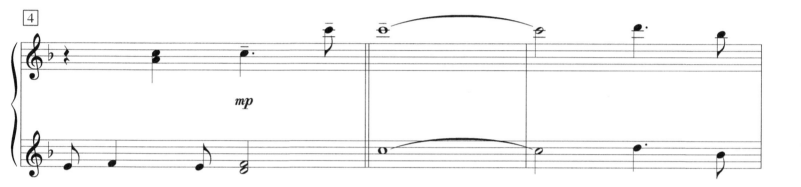

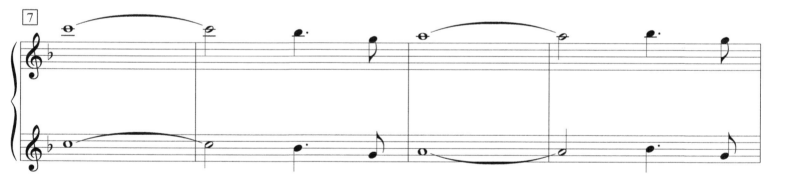

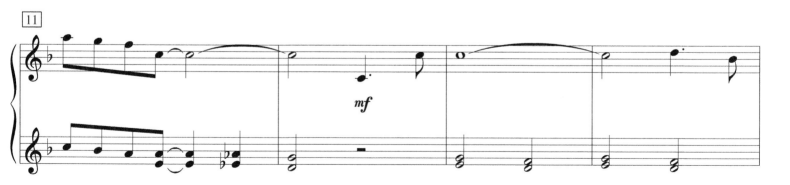

SECONDO

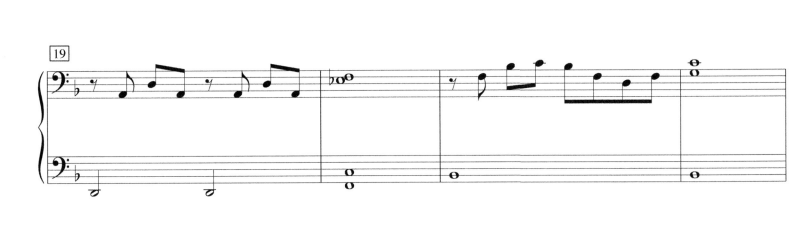

PRIMO

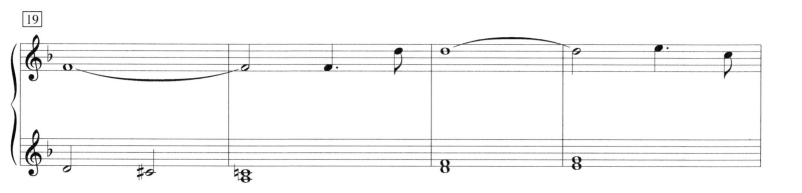

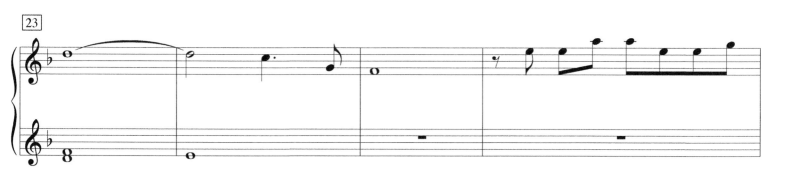

SECONDO

7

PRIMO

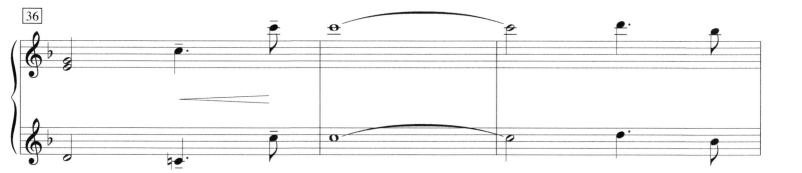

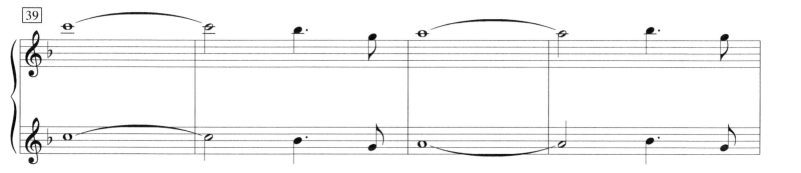

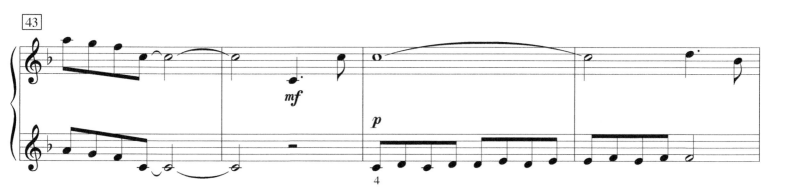

SECONDO

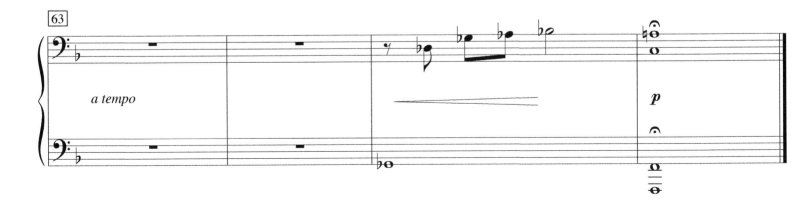

PRIMO

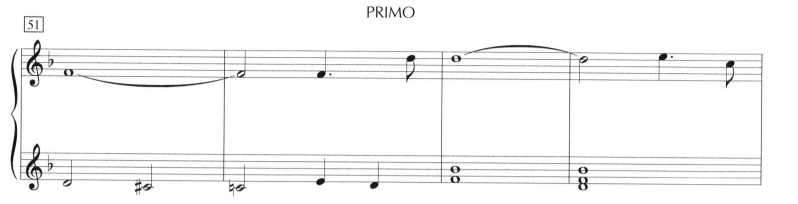

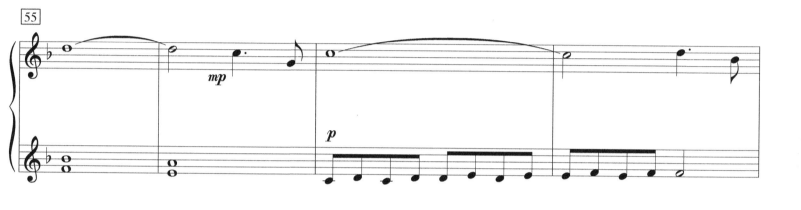

CASTLE ON A CLOUD

SECONDO

Music by CLAUDE-MICHEL SCHÖNBERG
Lyrics by ALAIN BOUBLIL,
JEAN-MARC NATEL and HERBERT KRETZMER

Slowly and smoothly

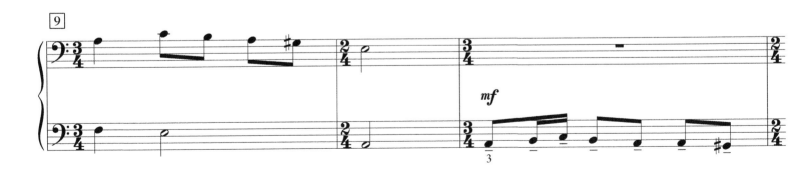

CASTLE ON A CLOUD

PRIMO

Music by CLAUDE-MICHEL SCHÖNBERG
Lyrics by ALAIN BOUBLIL,
JEAN-MARC NATEL and HERBERT KRETZMER

Slowly and smoothly

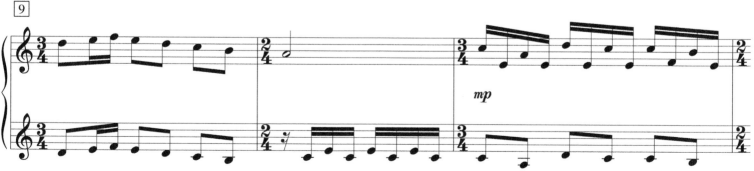

Music and French Lyrics Copyright © 1980 by Editions Musicales Alain Boublil
English Lyrics Copyright © 1986 by Alain Boublil Music Ltd. (ASCAP)
Mechanical and Publication Rights for the U.S.A. Administered by Alain Boublil Music Ltd. (ASCAP)
c/o Spielman Koenigsberg & Parker LLP, Richard Koenigsberg, 1745 Broadway, New York NY 10019, Tel 212-453-2500, Fax 212-453-2550, ABML@skpny.com

SECONDO

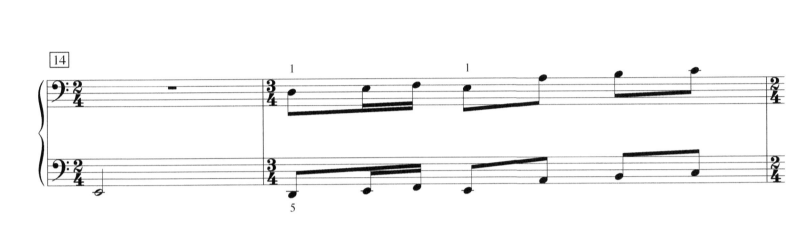

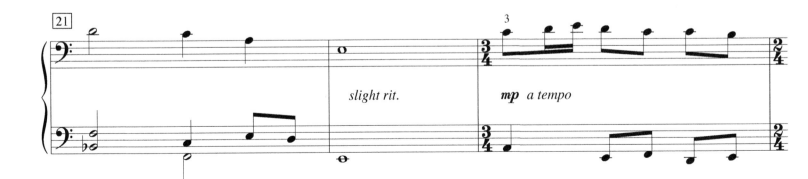

PRIMO

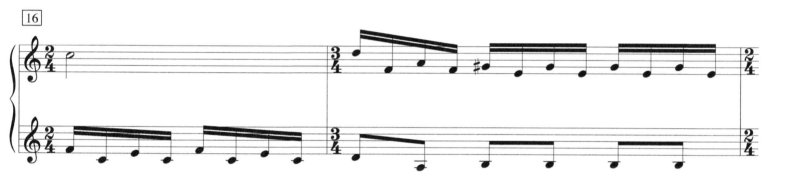

SECONDO

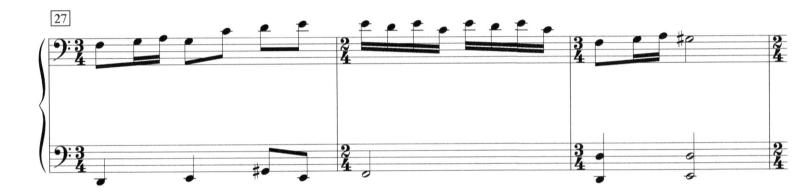

PRIMO

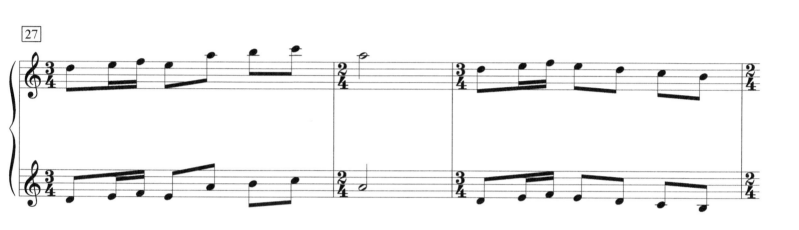

DO YOU HEAR THE PEOPLE SING?

SECONDO

Music by CLAUDE-MICHEL SCHÖNBERG
Lyrics by ALAIN BOUBLIL,
JEAN-MARC NATEL and HERBERT KRETZMER

DO YOU HEAR THE PEOPLE SING?

PRIMO

Music by CLAUDE-MICHEL SCHÖNBERG
Lyrics by ALAIN BOUBLIL,
JEAN-MARC NATEL and HERBERT KRETZMER

Grand March

SECONDO

PRIMO

SECONDO

PRIMO

A HEART FULL OF LOVE

SECONDO

Music by CLAUDE-MICHEL SCHÖNBERG
Lyrics by ALAIN BOUBLIL,
JEAN-MARC NATEL and HERBERT KRETZMER

Moderate Waltz

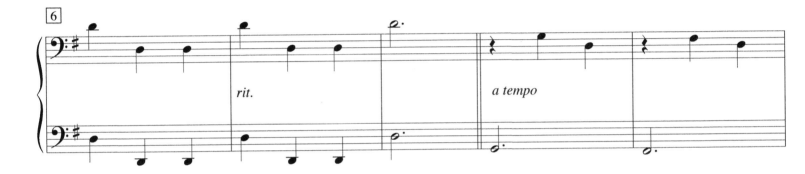

A HEART FULL OF LOVE

PRIMO

Music by CLAUDE-MICHEL SCHÖNBERG
Lyrics by ALAIN BOUBLIL,
JEAN-MARC NATEL and HERBERT KRETZMER

Moderate Waltz

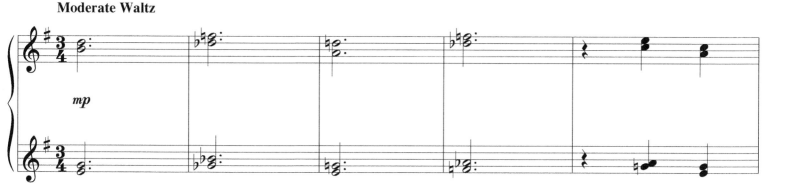

SECONDO

PRIMO

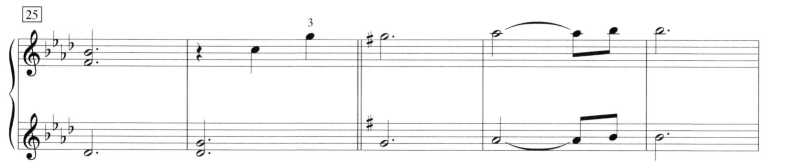

SECONDO

PRIMO

SECONDO

29

PRIMO

rit.

I DREAMED A DREAM

SECONDO

Music by CLAUDE-MICHEL SCHÖNBERG
Lyrics by ALAIN BOUBLIL,
JEAN-MARC NATEL and HERBERT KRETZMER

Andante, with expression

I DREAMED A DREAM

PRIMO

Music by CLAUDE-MICHEL SCHÖNBERG
Lyrics by ALAIN BOUBLIL,
JEAN-MARC NATEL and HERBERT KRETZMER

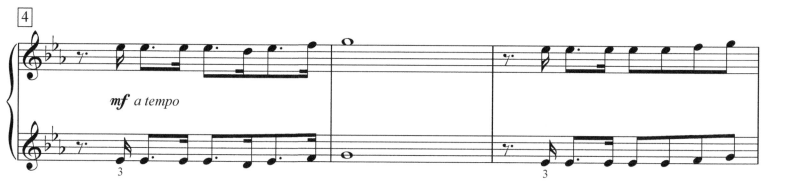

SECONDO

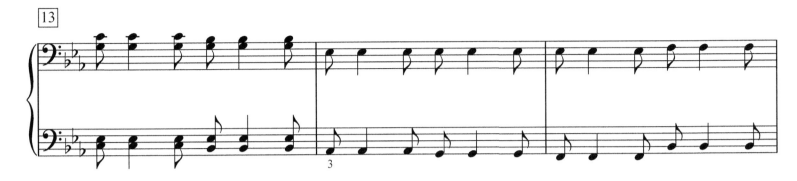

cresc. e rit.

PRIMO

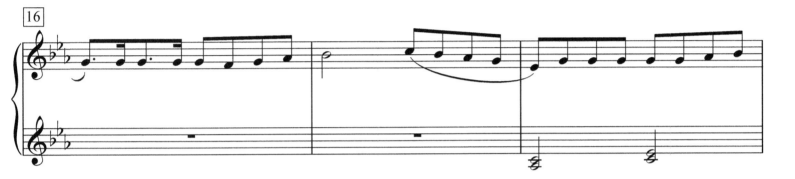

cresc. e rit.

PRIMO

SECONDO

PRIMO

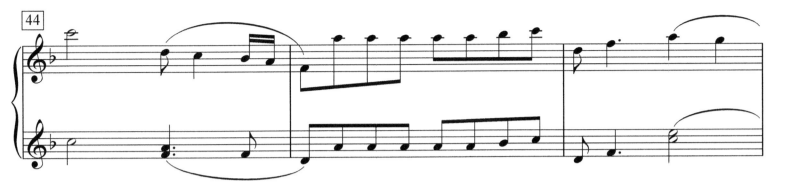

IN MY LIFE

SECONDO

Music by CLAUDE-MICHEL SCHÖNBERG
Lyrics by ALAIN BOUBLIL,
JEAN-MARC NATEL and HERBERT KRETZMER

Slowly, with expression

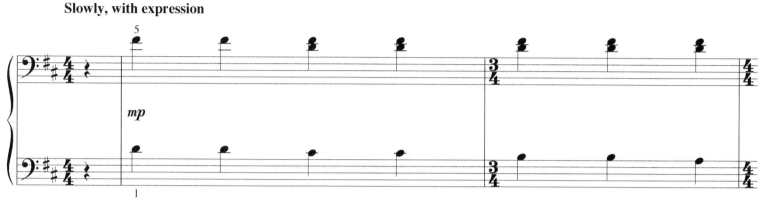

IN MY LIFE

PRIMO

Music by CLAUDE-MICHEL SCHÖNBERG
Lyrics by ALAIN BOUBLIL,
JEAN-MARC NATEL and HERBERT KRETZMER

Slowly, with expression

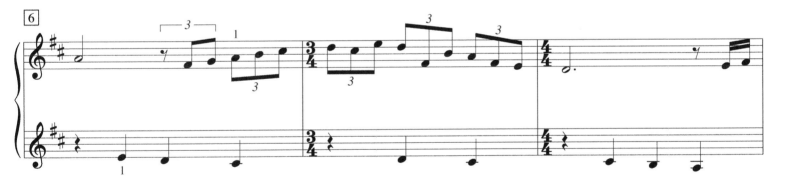

SECONDO

PRIMO

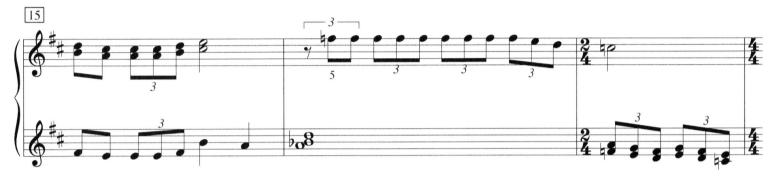

SECONDO

PRIMO

SECONDO

PRIMO

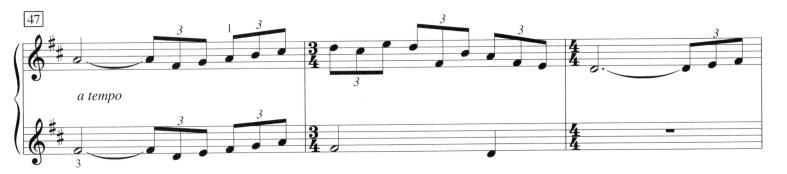

46

SECONDO

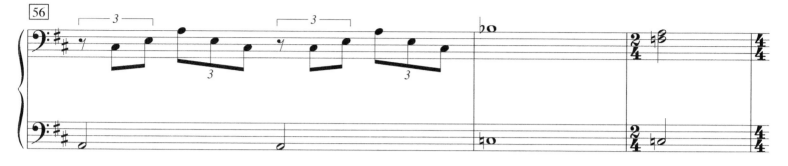

PRIMO

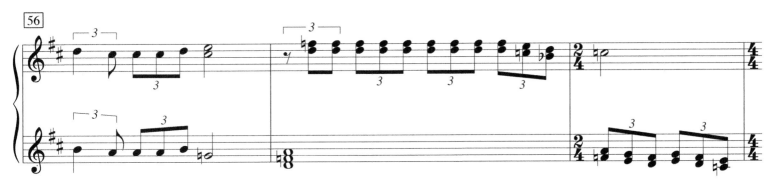

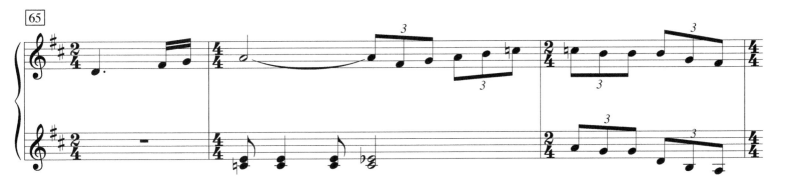

ON MY OWN

SECONDO

Music by CLAUDE-MICHEL SCHÖNBERG
Lyrics by ALAIN BOUBLIL, JEAN-MARC NATEL,
HERBERT KRETZMER, JOHN CAIRD and TREVOR NUNN

ON MY OWN

PRIMO

Music by CLAUDE-MICHEL SCHÖNBERG
Lyrics by ALAIN BOUBLIL, JEAN-MARC NATEL,
HERBERT KRETZMER, JOHN CAIRD and TREVOR NUNN

Andante (♩ = ca. 66)

SECONDO

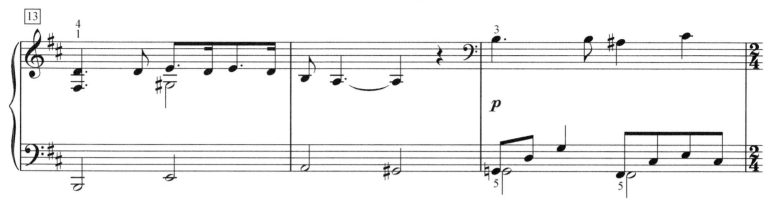

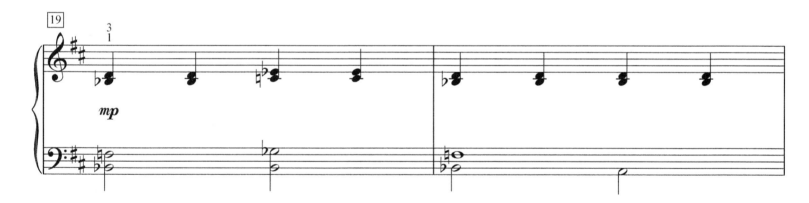

PRIMO

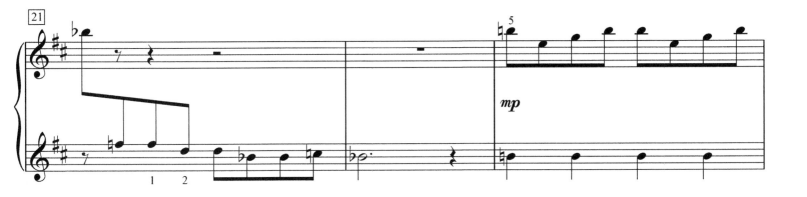

52

SECONDO

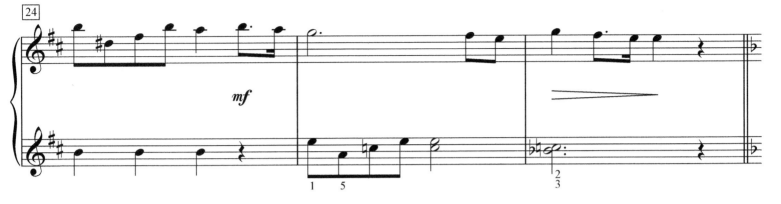

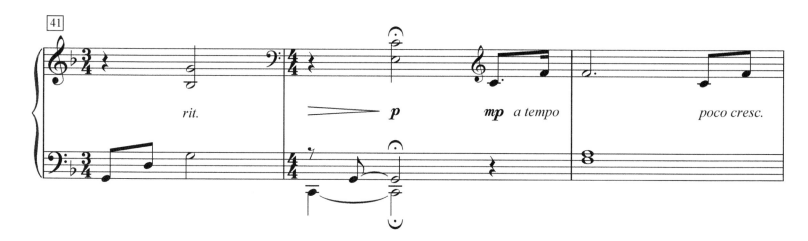

STARS

SECONDO

Music by CLAUDE-MICHEL SCHÖNBERG
Lyrics by HERBERT KRETZMER and ALAIN BOUBLIL

Smoothly and expressively

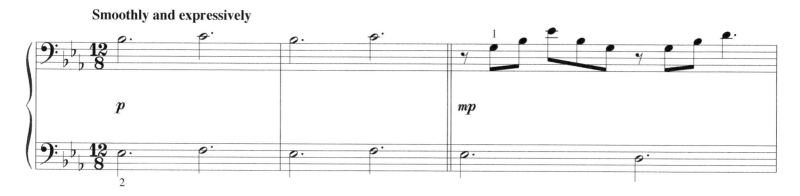

STARS

PRIMO

Music by CLAUDE-MICHEL SCHÖNBERG
Lyrics by HERBERT KRETZMER and ALAIN BOUBLIL

Smoothly and expressively

SECONDO

PRIMO

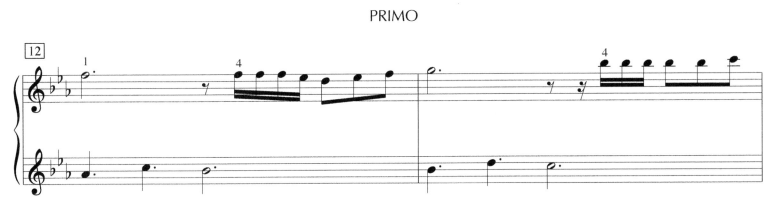

SECONDO

PRIMO

SECONDO

PRIMO

PIANO FOR TWO
A Variety of Piano Duets from Hal Leonard

ADELE FOR PIANO DUET
Intermediate Level

Eight of Adele's biggest hits arranged especially for intermediate piano duet! Featuring: Chasing Pavements • Hello • Make You Feel My Love • Rolling in the Deep • Set Fire to the Rain • Skyfall • Someone Like You • When We Were Young.

00172162 1 Piano, 4 Hands..............$14.99

THE BEATLES FOR PIANO DUET
Intermediate Level
arr. Eric Baumgartner

Eight great Beatles' songs arranged for piano duet! Titles: Blackbird • Come Together • In My Life • Lucy in the Sky with Diamonds • Michelle • Ob-la-di, Ob-la-da • While My Guitar Gently Weeps • Yellow Submarine.

00275877 1 Piano, 4 Hands $14.99

THE BIG BOOK OF PIANO DUETS

24 great piano duet arrangements! Includes: Beauty and the Beast • Clocks • Edelweiss • Georgia on My Mind • He's a Pirate • Let It Go • Linus and Lucy • Moon River • Yellow Submarine • You are the Sunshine of My Life • and more!

00232851 1 Piano, 4 Hands..............$17.99

CONTEMPORARY DISNEY DUETS
Intermediate Level

8 great Disney duets: Evermore (from Beauty and the Beast) • How Does a Moment Last Forever (from Beauty and the Beast) • How Far I'll Go (from Moana) • Lava • Let It Go (from Frozen) • Proud Corazon (from Coco) • Remember Me (from Coco) • You're Welcome (from Moana).

00285562 1 Piano, 4 Hands..............$12.99

EASY CLASSICAL DUETS
Book/Online Audio
Willis Music

7 great piano duets to perform at a recital, play-for-fun, or sightread: By the Beautiful Blue Danube (Strauss) • Eine kleine Nachtmusik (Mozart) • Hungarian Rhapsody No. 5 (Liszt) • Morning from Peer Gynt (Grieg) • Rondeau (Mouret) • Sleeping Beauty Waltz (Tchaikovsky) • Surprise Symphony (Haydn). Includes online audio tracks for the primo and secondo part for download or streaming.

00145767 1 Piano, 4 Hands..............$12.99

FAVORITE DISNEY SONGS FOR PIANO DUET
Early Intermediate Level

8 great Disney songs creatively arranged for piano duet: Can You Feel the Love Tonight • Do You Want to Build a Snowman • A Dream Is a Wish Your Heart Makes • Supercalifragilisticexpialidocious • That's How You Know • When Will My Life Begin? • You'll Be in My Heart • You've Got a Friend in Me.

00285563 1 Piano, 4 Hands..............$14.99

FIRST 50 PIANO DUETS YOU SHOULD PLAY

Includes: Autumn Leaves • Bridge over Troubled Water • Chopsticks • Fields of Gold • Hallelujah • Imagine • Lean on Me • Theme from "New York, New York" • Over the Rainbow • Peaceful Easy Feeling • Singin' in the Rain • A Thousand Years • What the World Needs Now Is Love • You Raise Me Up • and more.

00276571 1 Piano, 4 Hands..............$19.99

GOSPEL DUETS
The Phillip Keveren Series

Eight inspiring hymns arranged by Phillip Keveren for one piano, four hands, including: Church in the Wildwood • His Eye Is on the Sparrow • In the Garden • Just a Closer Walk with Thee • The Old Rugged Cross • Shall We Gather at the River? • There Is Power in the Blood • When the Roll Is Called up Yonder.

00295099 1 Piano, 4 Hands..............$12.99

THE GREATEST SHOWMAN
by Benj Pasek & Justin Paul
Intermediate Level

Creative piano duet arrangements for the songs: Come Alive • From Now On • The Greatest Show • A Million Dreams • Never Enough • The Other Side • Rewrite the Stars • This Is Me • Tightrope.

00295078 1 Piano, 4 Hands..............$16.99

BILLY JOEL FOR PIANO DUET
Intermediate Level

8 of the Piano Man's greatest hits – perfect as recital encores, or just for fun! Titles: It's Still Rock and Roll to Me • Just the Way You Are • The Longest Time • My Life • New York State of Mind • Piano Man • She's Always a Woman • Uptown Girl.

00141139 1 Piano, 4 Hands..............$14.99

HEART AND SOUL & OTHER DUET FAVORITES

8 fun duets arranged for two people playing on one piano. Includes: Any Dream Will Do • Chopsticks • Heart and Soul • Music! Music! Music! (Put Another Nickel In) • On Top of Spaghetti • Raiders March • The Rainbow Connection • Y.M.C.A..

00290541 1 Piano, 4 Hands..............$12.99

RHAPSODY IN BLUE
George Gershwin/ arr. Brent Edstrom

Originally written for piano and jazz band, "Rhapsody in Blue" was later orchestrated by Ferde Grofe. This intimate adaptation for piano duet delivers access to advancing pianists and provides an exciting musical collaboration and adventure!

00125150 1 Piano, 4 Hands..............$14.99

RIVER FLOWS IN YOU & OTHER SONGS FOR PIANO DUET
Intermediate Level

10 great songs including the title song and: All of Me (Piano Guys) • Bella's Lullaby • Beyond • Chariots of Fire • Dawn • Forrest Gump - Main Title (Feather Theme) • Primavera • Somewhere in Time • Watermark.

00141055 1 Piano, 4 Hands..............$12.99

TOP HITS FOR EASY PIANO DUET
Book/Online Audio
arr. David Pearl

10 great songs with backing tracks: Despacito (Justin Bieber ft. Luis Fonsi & Daddy Yankee) • Havana (Camila Cabello ft. Young Thug • High Hopes (Panic! At the Disco) • A Million Dreams (*The Greatest Showman*) • Perfect (Ed Sheeran) • Senorita (Camila Cabello & Shawn Mendes) • Shallow (Lady Gaga & Bradley Cooper) • Someone You Loved (Lewis Capaldi) • Speechless (*Aladdin*) • Sucker (Jonas Brothers).

00326133 1 Piano, 4 Hands..............$12.99

HAL•LEONARD®
www.halleonard.com

0325
05-